Just a very small Token for Carolyn – in order
to say "thank you" for many beautiful days
and experiences in her wonderful home-
country, – and again we express our
sincere hope to see her in Austria <u>yearly</u> !!!

God bless you!

Hedi WITH LOVE!!!

Liebe Carolyn, zur Erinnerung an unsere gemeinsamen Ferien
in Deinem schönen Heimatland, das wir dank Deiner Fürsorge
in all seiner Schönheit kennenlernen durften.
 Danke, danke, danke!
  In Liebe
   Eva

UTAH

UTAH

Photography by
FLOYD HOLDMAN
Text by
NELSON WADSWORTH

SKYLINE
PRESS

Produced by Roger Boulton Publishing Services, Toronto
Designed by Fortunato Aglialoro
© 1984 Oxford University Press (Canadian Branch)
SKYLINE PRESS is a registered imprint of Oxford University Press
ISBN 0-19-540602-8
1 2 3 4 – 7 6 5 4

Printed in Hong Kong by Scanner Art Services, Inc., Toronto

INTRODUCTION

'You can spend your whole life exploring the Colorado Plateau and the wilderness of Utah, and when you're through you've only scratched the surface. There's just too much for one man to see and do in a lifetime.'

The speaker was old 'Doc' A.L. Inglesby, sitting amid the backyard clutter of his rockshop in the sleepy little town of Fruita, a quarter of a century ago. Above him rose the blazing red sandstone cliffs of Capitol Reef. Outside the gate the bumpy dirt road twisted down into Capitol Gorge. Motorists were often stranded in Fruita then by the violent flash-floods that swept through the Gorge in late summer, but the town was also famous for its balmy desert air and the orchards that thrived in the long growing season. People came from miles around for the cherries, peaches, apricots, apples and pears.

When Doc Inglesby said that no one lifetime could ever be enough for the knowledge and appreciation of Utah, he knew what he was talking about. Indeed, he had spent the whole of his life courting Utah's majesty. He leaned back in his rickety wooden chair, took a well-chewed cigar from his nearly toothless mouth, scratched his whiskered chin, and his eyes wandered reflectively over the chunks of petrified wood, dinosaur bones, polished and unpolished gemstones winking in the clear desert sunlight that filtered through the shade trees. These mounds of fossils, rocks and crystals picked up around the dusty back trails, in the mines, the canyons and the desert, were the accumulation of his years. Yet now, in old age, he would only admit to having 'scratched the surface'.

When he died at the age of 87 in 1960, Doc's collections were given to the Utah Museum of Natural History. Similarly in 1967 his friend Charles Kelly bequeathed a lifetime of historical research, books, paintings and artefacts to the Utah Historical Society and the University of Utah. But these two men left another legacy that was perhaps even more important. Together they had done a great deal to foster the appreciation of Utah's unique variety. Charles Kelly, a historian who wrote historical novels in his spare time, had been the first superintendent of parks and was the pioneer superintendent of Capitol Reef. Doc Inglesby organized and advocated 'Intelligence Tours' of Utah's natural wonders, providing bus services and guided tours in the 1920's and early 1930's from Salt Lake City to Zion and Bryce Canyons, Cedar Breaks and other attractions throughout the state. They wanted to open up the wild and lonely deserts, the massive stone Canyonlands, the snow-capped mountain wilderness, in order that people should better understand and appreciate these awesome, infinite wonders. Where else, Doc and Kelly would often say, could one find such physical contrasts? Indeed, where else, we may now ask, can one explore such shores as those of the Western Hemisphere's largest, inland 'dead sea', and the next day climb through evergreen forests to a 13,500 ft dome like King's Peak? Where else can one play in the tepid waters of a 186-mile man-made lake in a desert oasis and next day fish for trout in cold lakes high above timberline?

An incredible variety of physiographic features is concentrated in the 85,000 square miles that comprise the State of Utah. To the west, the Great Basin Province sprawls for endless miles of sage-covered deserts and intermittent, rocky peaks. To the east, the vast chasms of the Canyonlands lace the Colorado Plateau Province with their towering standing rocks and great, natural skyscrapers of eroded stone. The mighty Colorado River and its tributaries twist their way through this maze of sedimentary sand, angrily seeking an outlet to the sea. To the north, and through the central axis of the state, the rugged Wasatch and Uinta Mountains loom above pristine, evergreen forests, plush green meadows and alpine canyons, in the long, wide fingers of the Rocky Mountain Province.

A prime example of Utah's 'geological textbook' can be found between Vernal and Flaming Gorge on the Red Cloud Scenic Loop. This 79-mile stretch of highway climbs up out of the Uinta Basin into Ashley National Forest, traversing a billion years of Earth's history and giving travelers a 'Drive Through the Ages'. As the road climbs higher, each geologic formation and its age is labeled by a sign.

Vernal is also the jumping-off place for Dinosaur National Monument, where rich beds of dinosaur bone are still quarried. Since 1916, some of the world's most spectacular dinosaur skeletons have been unearthed in Utah, most specimens being taken from 'digs' at Dinosaur National Monument near Jensen in the northeastern part of the state and at Cleveland-Lloyd Quarry in Emery County. More complete skeletons of a wide variety of prehistoric reptiles have been recovered from these two quarries than from any other sites in the world. Among them were several well-preserved specimens of the ferocious *Allosaurus*, a carnivorous reptile that lived in Utah 150 million years ago. Palaeontologists from the Carnegie Museum, the American Museum of Natural History, the University of Utah, Princeton University, Brigham Young University and other leading institutions have found rich deposits of dinosaur bones in Utah. Many of these bones have been reassembled and mounted for display in museums from Milan, Italy, to Osaka, Japan. The great reptiles that thrived in the age of dinosaurs dominated life in Utah longer than any other creatures in the animal kingdom. *Homo sapiens* is a relative newcomer.

Hogup Cave, in the rocky escarpments along the hot, desolate northwestern shore of the Great Salt Lake, has provided archaeologists with a near perfect record of human occupancy from Mesolithic man up to the Indian cultures that were living in the Great Basin when the white man arrived. Thousands of artefacts, such as pieces of woven reed matting, remnants of elk-tooth necklaces, flint knives, bone awls, have been dated from 6400 BC to about AD 1800, giving historians a wealth of clues about the life of early man in Western America, and revealing evidence of continuous human habitation in this remote wasteland, from the early Stone Age to the Shoshoni Indians of relatively recent times.

Hogup Cave lies about 75 miles northwest of Salt Lake City, overlooking an arm of the glistening white Salt Flats, some 55 miles from the world-famous Bonneville Speedway. There is probably not a more inhospitable stretch of geography in North America. Yet primitive Utah people, possibly among the first men in North America, foraged for food here nearly 10,000 years ago.

Artefacts from Hogup, and those unearthed at the earlier Danger Cave near Wendover, give anthropologists a fairly clear picture of the lifestyles of the early Desert Archaic, Fremont and Plains Indian cultures.

These American aborigines were the forerunners of the later Pueblo Cliff Dwellers who profusely inhabited the Colorado Plateau between AD 400 and the 13th century. Hundreds of ruins still stand in scattered parts of the Plateau Province, the last remnants of an advanced agricultural society that flourished and then mysteriously vanished sometime in the late 1200s. Anthropologists, studying tree-ring clues, surmise that a great drought made the Colorado Plateau too arid for human occupation and the culture, which depended on the harvest, shrank, eventually evolving into the current Pueblo, Zuni, Hopi and Navajo tribes of today. The Navajos call the people of this prehistoric culture the 'Anasazi' or 'Ancient Ones'.

Prime examples of the Anasazi civilization are still extant in Utah in Canyonlands National Park, Lake Powell National Recreation Area, Capitol Reef National Park, and throughout San Juan, Emery, Grand, Garfield, Wayne and Kane Counties. But probably the most spectacular can be found at Hovenweep National Monument south of Monticello near the Aneth Oil Field. Six impressive groups of ancient Pueblo ruins, similar in nature to those at Mesa Verde in Colorado to the east, still survive. The complex was abandoned between 700 and 800 years ago.

The aboriginal peoples of Utah also left behind examples of their creativity, not only in fine, oven-fired pottery, but in chipped and painted rock art. Excellent examples of petroglyphs (chipped art in stone) and pictographs (painted pigments on stone) can be found in nearly every county. Probably the best known, however, are in Canyonlands National Park. Newspaper Rock, as it is called, contains numerous figures and designs chipped by Indian artists on a sandstone wall. In Horsehoe Canyon, near Robber's Roost, a giant mural of Indian figures is painted in broad strokes with ochre on the sheer canyon wall. The Horsehoe Canyon painter, obviously gifted in his art, also executed scenes of an antelope hunt in which figures carrying *atlatls* (throwing sticks) are about to attack their prey.

When the Horsehoe Canyon painter was spreading his ochre on the canyon wall, white men were unknown in Utah. Palefaces did not arrive on the scene until the 18th century, when two Catholic monks made their way through the Wasatch Mountains looking for a route from the Spanish mission at Santa Fe to Monterey on the West Coast. The priest-explorers, Fathers Dominguez and Escalante, followed established trails north through Colorado, avoided the forbidding Canyonlands region, entered Utah east of what later would become Vernal, crossed the Green River and headed west through the Wasatch to Utah Valley. They looked down for the first time at Utah Lake in 1776, the year of American Independence.

After spending some time with the Timpanogos Ute Indians who lived near the lake, Escalante decided to abandon his search for a route to Monterey, and the party set out by direct route back to Santa Fe. This was almost a fatal mistake because it led the expedition through unknown, treacherous cliff and canyon country along the Colorado River. The party nearly starved to death and suffered many hardships before it found a safe crossing near Glen Canyon. The site, known as Crossing of the Fathers, is now covered by hundreds of feet of water in Lake Powell behind Glen Canyon Dam.

As far as is known, no other white men set foot in Utah until fur trappers began harvesting their pelts from the environment in the 1820s. Etienne Provost is believed to have been the first white man to look on the Great Salt Lake, and Jim Bridger is first credited with tasting its salty water and navigating its brine in a boat in the fall of 1824. But it was not until the 1840s that the first wagon trains of emigrants made their way through Utah and blazed the trails to the West Coast, and it was not until 1847 that the first permanent white settlers put down their roots and firmly planted the American empire.

In July of that year a small, covered carriage could have been seen bouncing slowly over the clumps of sagebrush and wending its way through the thick foliage beside a swift mountain stream. Time and again it crossed the creek, back and forth, as the driver and oxen searched for the easiest passage. Finally, the vehicle climbed the slopes of a steep mountain and rolled to a stop on a bench just over the crest. The driver maneuvered his oxen into a tight turn, so that the open canvas flap of the carriage could face toward the western horizon. Then he spoke softly to a solitary figure lying on a mattress inside. The figure, a man in his mid-40s, stirred, turned on one side and looked out at the vast panorama that stretched below. With some difficulty, he rose from his bed, climbed down from the wagon, stood in a clearing surrounded by sagebrush, and scanned the horizon.

'It is enough,' he said at last. 'This is the right place, drive on!'

No book about Utah can be written without telling how Brigham Young and his Mormon Pioneers looked down for the first time on their new mountain and desert home. Their prophet's utterance at mid-day on the 24th of July 1847 that 'This is the Place!' has been a rallying cry and a source of pride for members of this religious faith ever since that memorable day, when Young, sick with mountain fever and weary from the long journey from Nebraska, halted his Pioneers along the shores of the Great Salt Lake and set about, as they said, 'to make the desert blossom as a rose'.

Utah was at the time a rugged, unexplored wilderness, inhabited by Indians, and a place that no one except the Indians really wanted. Yet it was ideal for the Mormon refugees, fleeing from persecution in Ohio, Missouri and Illinois at the hands of people who did not understand their religion. In this desert isolation the Mormons, or Latter-day Saints as they prefer to call themselves, were able to settle, establish commerce and ultimately prosper, despite an arid, unpredictable and often hostile environment.

Under the leadership of Brigham Young and other men of vision, the Mormons were able to colonize Utah and her surrounding states and leave behind a rich heritage. Their history is readily discernible to the modern-day traveler in a wealth of monuments and pioneer architecture. The Mormon Temple and Tabernacle in Salt Lake City, which took the Pioneers more than 40 years to build, are probably the most outstanding examples, along with others in St George, Manti and Logan, and their modern-day counterparts in Provo, Ogden and West

Jordan.

The Mormon monuments for the most part commemorate the travails of the Pioneers as they struggled to establish their Zion in the tops of the mountains...the invasion of crickets and the subsequent rescue of the crops by flocks of seagulls, the Handcart Pioneers who walked across the plains pushing and pulling their belongings in small, crude, wooden carts, and the men, women and events that played their parts in the history of the Latter-day Saints.

Mormons today comprise about 60 percent of the Utah population, which in 1964 passed the million mark and in the last decennial census was nearly 1.5 million. The state is still predominately rural, with 75 percent of the population living less than 50 miles from Salt Lake City, along the thickly-populated Wasatch Front.

East of the population centers the mountains act like magnets to the storms that move frequently through this region from the Pacific Ocean and the Gulf of Mexico, bringing snows in winter and thundershowers in summer. Because of its unique weather patterns, Utah enjoys some of the best skiing in the world, and the winter snows of Alta, just east of Salt Lake City, offer the finest powder skiing known. Yet the warm waters of Lake Powell in southern Utah, at ideal swimming temperature most of the year, offer some of the best water skiing to be enjoyed anywhere.

Because Utah is primarily a public domain state (that is to say most of its land is preserved by the federal government), exploitation is not as prevalent as in other states. National parks, forests and monuments have set aside the scenic wonders and valuable resources, the historical landmarks and the natural terrain, and have kept them from private ownership. Thus, everywhere at hand, the modern traveler encounters well-preserved evidence of the history of Mormon colonization, as well as the struggles of subsequent settlers to develop and improve the state's agriculture, mine her resources and establish her commerce. These moments of history are easily relived because, for the most part, the sites remain unchanged.

North of the Great Salt Lake, for example, where the Golden Spike was driven, the barren, wind-swept sageflats are still much the same as they were on the 10th of May 1869, when America was linked with steel by its first transcontinental railroad. Replicas of the coal-burning 'Engine 119' and the wood-burning 'Jupiter' re-enact the historic 'wedding of the rails', on a regular basis, on the exact spot where the original Golden Spike was driven.

In southern Utah, at Robber's Roost, where Butch Cassidy and the Sundance Kid hid from the law officers, and where Zane Grey got much of the background inspiration for his western novels, the forbidding canyons remain untouched and still guard their cowboy mysteries. The ghosts of colorful bandits still ride the Outlaw Trail. The ghosts of coal, copper and silver miners still haunt the many mining camps that boomed and busted when Utah tapped her mineral wealth and shipped it by railroad to the waiting markets of the world. Many of these ghost towns still stand, but the weathered wood, rusting steel and crumbling foundations speak of an early return to the desert elements from which they sprang. The ghost towns, the outlaw hide-aways, the Indian ruins, the dinosaur digs, the Mormon history, the magnificent natural wonders, all beckon to us, just as they did to Doc Inglesby, Charles Kelly and thousands of other modern-day explorers who have, like phantom figures, come and gone, but whose legacy remains and flourishes in our love and knowledge of Utah.

The old Doc took out the well-chewed cigar for the last time, looked at it wryly, and threw it in a nearby trashcan. He leaned back again in his rickety chair and smiled. His eyes were drawn once more to the desert light, filtering through the shade trees, and up to the sandstone cliffs beyond.

'Yes,' he said, 'maybe that's all a man can hope to do with a lifetime in Utah,—just scratch the surface. But I'll tell you this—the pleasure he gets from scratching will last forever.'

Logan, Utah, 1984 NELSON WADSWORTH

1 A thin band of cloud shrouds Squaw Peak just east of Provo, giving hint of an approaching storm. The peak is part of the Wasatch Mountain Range.

2 *(left)* Lightning crackles through the sky above Provo during a spectacular mid-summer electrical storm. Utah is noted for its changeable weather patterns.

3 The imposing statue of 'The Christus', by Danish sculptor Bertal Thorvaldsen, looms above the atrium in the Visitor's Center on Temple Square in Salt Lake City.

4 *(left)* A colorful display of clouds, warmed by the dying sun, unfolds over central Utah skies. The Beehive State is noted for its sunsets and cloud formations.

5 A crescent moon adorns the summer sky over the jagged cliffs of Zion National Park, one of eight national parks and monuments in Utah.

6 An early morning sun backlights Rainbow Bridge, the largest natural bridge in the world. Reflection of the 308-foot-high span shimmers in man-made Lake Powell.

7 *(right)* Hikers pause in a shaft of sunlight beaming through Jacob Hamblin Arch in Coyote Gulch near the Escalante River. The arch is named after an early Mormon explorer who befriended the southern Utah Indians.

8 The hot winds of Juab County create unique, shifting mounds of sand in the Little Sahara Desert in west central Utah. The region is a favourite haunt for dune buggies and four-wheel-drive enthusiasts.

9 (right) The sheer cliffs of Wild Horse Mesa dwarf eroded desert sandhills in southeastern Utah. Herds of wild horses once thrived in this region.

10 A Utah quail peeks from stalks of dry wheat in the flat farmlands of central Utah. The area is noted for its pheasant and quail hunting.

11 *(right)* Hikers inspect the painted pictographs of Utah's ancient Fremont Indians near Robber's Roost in southeastern Utah. The primitive art, done in native ochre pigment, dates between AD 500 and AD 1200.

12 *(left)* A late afternoon sun brings desert grasses to life beneath the cliffs of Monument Valley near Four Corners, where the borders of four states join.

13 A Crow Indian child, dressed in traditional finery, sits tall in the saddle prior to a Pow Wow in Springville. Utah is rich in Indian lore and history.

14 The unique, eroded shapes of Goblin Valley, near Robber's Roost, stand silently, as if in military formation. Indians feared this region because of its ghostly shapes.

15 (right) A full moon rises over the sandstone cliffs near Hanksville, one of Utah's most rugged, isolated and thinly populated wilderness regions.

16 *(left)* The moon rises over the 'Mittens' in Monument Valley near the Four Corners. The region is home of the proud Navajo Indian and his native culture.

17 A clump of quaking aspen trees flourishes on the slopes of Boulder Mountain. The trees, widespread in Utah mountains, are named for their unique leaves which 'quake' in the spring, summer and fall breezes.

18 A 20th century 'mountain man' dresses in native furs for a modern-day 'rendez-vous'. History buffs re-enact early fur-trapper lifestyles.

19 *(right)* Mt Timpanogos backdrops the deep, powdery snow of the Wasatch Mountains. Powder skiing in this range is deemed among the best in the world.

20 *(left)* A unique rock formation called 'The Molar' frames Angel Arch in Canyonlands National Park. The 'angel', with bowed head and folded wings, is a key attraction of the park.

21 Hikers make their way along the shore of the Escalante River in a wilderness area of south central Utah. Much of the lower Escalante, a tributary of the Colorado River, is inundated by man-made Lake Powell Reservoir.

22 'The Hunter', a formation in Bryce Canyon, overlooks the distant slopes of the Aquarius Plateau, one of the highest conifer forests in the world.

23 *(right)* A vast amphitheater of eroded stone unfolds from Utah's Markagunt Plateau in the southeastern part of the state. The half-mile-deep natural wonder has been set aside as Cedar Breaks National Monument.

24 Glistening white salt flats surround one of the major islands in the Great Salt Lake, America's vast, inland 'dead sea'. The lake is similar to the Dead Sea in the Holy Land.

25 Winter clouds swirl around the slopes of Mt Timpanogos, one of Utah's more prominent mountain peaks. The mountain stands 11,750 feet above sea level and is visible throughout much of central Utah.

26 'Quarry' of dinosaur bones at Dinosaur National Monument near Jensen.

27 *(right)* The fractured stone of Stevens or 'Skyline' Arch rises above the Escalante River in southeastern Utah. The waters of Lake Powell Reservoir behind Glen Canyon Dam have backed up the Escalante to a point just below Stevens Canyon.

28 (left) Hovenweep Castle, one of the best-preserved and most extensive Indian ruins in Utah, overlooks Ruin Canyon in southeastern Utah. The culture that built Hovenweep is similar to that of Mesa Verde in Colorado to the east.

29 Calf Creek Falls cascade down the slickrock in Calf Creek Canyon, not far from the creek's confluence with the Escalante River. Two series of falls create pools of clear water in this desert oasis.

30 *(left)* Slate grey buttes rise above the desert floor near Capitol Reef National Monument in southcentral Utah. The strange cloud formation is merely a passing cumulus cloud, typical in the dry, desert environment.

31 Hikers inspect the entrance to the Hole-in-the-Rock near the Colorado River, where Mormon Pioneers blasted and chiseled a notch in the sandstone in 1879 to lower their wagons down to cross the river.

32 An appropriate series of clouds accents 'The Smokestacks in the Fiery Furnace' at Arches National Park near Moab. Some of the world's most spectacular natural formations can be found in this region.

33 Colored sandstone domes and pinnacles rim Chesler Park in Canyonlands
National Park, world famous for its silent 'cities of stone'.

34 *(left)* Backlight from the sun brings a clump of cottonwood trees to life in Canyonlands National Park. The deep-rooted cottonwood is one of the few species of trees that can survive in the harsh desert environment.

35 Water cascades over lava stone in Deep Creek in the Deep Creek Mountains of western Utah near Fish Springs.

36 A two-tiered cataract plunges down the face of
Cascade Mountain into the Provo River in Utah
County, forming the beautiful tresses of Bridal Veil
Falls.

37 *(right)* The deep gorge of the upper Escalante
River begins its descent from the Aquarius Plateau
toward the Colorado River in southcentral Utah.

38 *(left)* The eroded mounds of Factory Butte serve as a unique landmark in the desert between Cainsville and Hanksville in Wayne County.

39 A pristine lake seething with trout is just one of thousands nestled on the slopes of the High Uinta Mountains, America's only major mountain chain running east and west.

40 *(left)* Paprika-colored sandstone cliffs jut upward along the edge of Highway 24 in Capitol Reef National Park near Fruita.

41 Bright red blooms peek out between the thorns of desert hedgehog cacti in Utah's Canyonlands. The plant is sometimes called 'winecup' or 'goblet' cactus.

42 *(left)* Mist shrouds a snow-capped peak in the Wasatch Mountains near Sundance Ski Resort. The Wasatch Range is part of Utah's rocky Mountain Province.

43 A patina of snow frosts the evergreens in the Wasatch Mountains on the slopes of Sundance Ski Resort near the Alpine Loop in central Utah.

44 Lava stone is strewn on the slopes of vari-colored mounds in Capitol Reef National Park, leaving evidence of prehistoric volcanic eruptions.

45 *(right)* Purple plateaux enhance the backdrop of Canyonlands in southeastern Utah. Vari-colored slickrock formations make the area a photographer's paradise.

46 *(left)* Brigham Young University students re-enact the trek of the Mormon Handcart Pioneers who pushed and pulled small wooden carts to Utah in the late 1850s.

47 Pristine evergreen forests thrive on the slopes of Boulder Mountain on the Aquarius Plateau. In the distance are red-rock deserts and the Henry Mountains.

48 An old abandoned shack still stands near Moab, giving evidence of early-day
homesteading and prospecting for minerals in the harsh desert.

49 A large rock seems to defy gravity in Arches National Park near Moab. Known
as 'Balancing Rock', the formation is one of many natural sculptures in the park.

50 Wooden houses in the old mining town of Park City tell of the lifestyles of Utah silver miners. The town is a popular tourist attraction east of Salt Lake City.

51 *(right)* Horses graze in a pasture in front of a white-washed farmhouse in Boulder. The little cluster of houses sits on the lower slopes of the Aquarius Plateau.

52 A huge painted mural in the Union Pacific Railroad Station in Salt Lake City depicts the arrival of Brigham Young and the Mormon Pioneers in the Valley in 1847.

53 *(right)* The golden statue of the Angel Moroni stands with trump in hand atop the Mormon Temple in Salt Lake City; in the foreground is the statue of Brigham Young.

54 *(left)* The warm afternoon sun gives a glow to the spires of the Egyptian Temple in Capitol Reef National Park near Fruita.

55 Lush green pastures in Utah County are backdropped by the snow-capped peak of Mt Timpanogos which looms above the valley floor.

56 Cattle graze in the pastures beneath Mt Nebo, a snow-covered peak in the Wasatch Range. Mt Nebo rises 11,928 feet above sea level and is another massif like Mt Timpanogos.

57 and 58 The Capitol Dome *(right)* and the Capitol Gorge *(overleaf)* are principal features of Capitol Reef National Park in Wayne County.

58 Capitol Gorge.

59 *(right)* The harsh colors of grey and red sandstone create a distinctive landscape near Mexican Hat, located in the narrow gorge of the San Juan River.

60 A hiker pauses in the dry wash near Horseshoe Canyon, not far from Robber's Roost and the tiny settlement of Hanksville.

61 (right) The 'Totem Poles' of Monument Valley overlook the red sand mounds of the desert near Four Corners, where Utah, Arizona, New Mexico and Colorado touch their borders.

62 and 63 Zion National Park: A spring-fed desert swimming hole *(left)*, lends a refreshing pause for summer hikers. Cottonwood trees *(right)* line the Virgin River after it emerges from Zion Narrows.

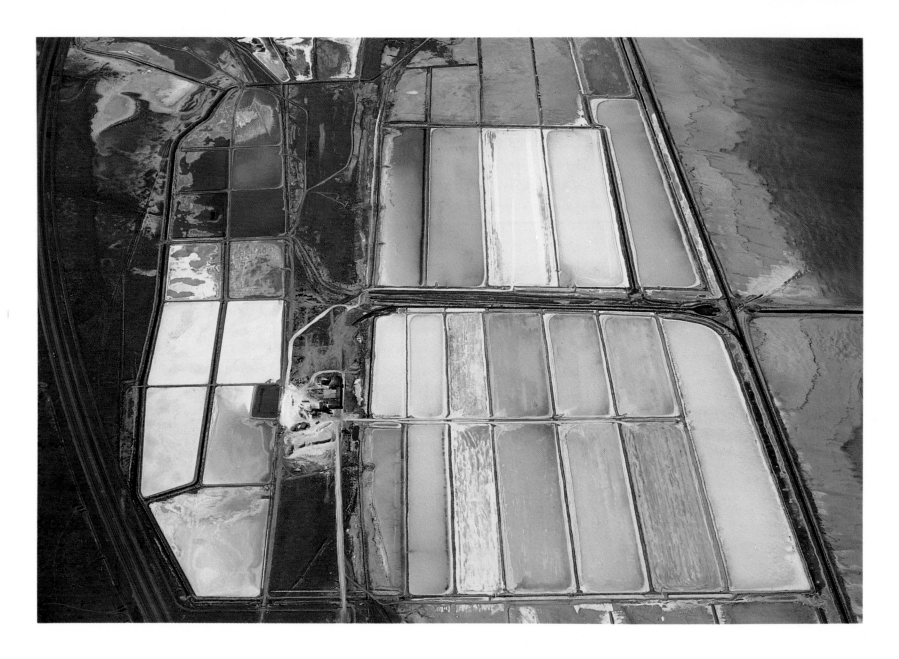

64 Brine-settling ponds create a quilt-like pattern along the shores of the Great Salt Lake, where industry extracts a variety of minerals, ranging from magnesium to common table salt.

65 *(right)* The multi-terraced Kennecott Copper Mine is one of the largest and most famous man-made excavations in the world. Copper ore is blasted from this huge hole, now more than a half-mile deep, two miles across and visible by satellite from outer space.

66 *(left)* The 'Silent City' of Bryce Canyon lifts its pink and white spires toward the sky on the eastern edge of the Paunsaugunt Plateau in southwestern Utah.

67 The antique white oolitic limestone walls of the magnificent Manti Temple in Sanpete County overlook the little central Utah Mormon settlement. The Temple was completed in 1888.

68 (left) 'Park Avenue' in Arches National Park lends a sophisticated air to Utah's red-rock wilderness near Moab.

69 'Fat Man's Misery' is the name of a narrow canyon in Robber's Roost, of Butch Cassidy fame. One hiker demonstrates the distance between the walls of the deep crevice.

70 A fountain plays in the quad of the modern Dixie College campus in St George.
This region is called 'Utah's Dixie'.

71 The magnificent, beautifully landscaped St George Temple was the first to be
completed in Utah. It was dedicated in 1877.

72 The placid waters of Lake Powell lap the red sandstone cliffs behind Glen Canyon Dam, creating a huge, 180-mile-long body of water with nearly 1,900 miles of shoreline.

73 *(right)* The Carillon Bell Tower and the Monte Bean Life Sciences Museum at Brigham Young University are nestled beneath Mt Timpanogos in Utah County. The University, with 25,000 students, is the largest private institution of higher learning in the world.

74 Shadowy peaks of the Wasatch Range loom above the lush pastures of Heber Valley, noted for its dairy herds and milk products.

75 *(right)* A single-engine airplane wends its way over the updrafts of the Wasatch Range. Below, the foliage has already started to explode into fall color.

76 *(left)* Desert sage flats stretch for many miles in southeastern Utah, with the sandstone cliffs of the Canyonlands Province rising in the background.

77 The waters of Lake Powell create a boater's paradise for water skiers, swimmers, fishermen and sunbathers.

78 The Church Office Building, Salt Lake City.

79 *(right)* Ducks waddle along a pond in Utah Valley as mist shrouds the snowy slopes of Mt Nebo.

80 A kaleidoscope of color emerges from the flowerbeds on Temple Square in Salt Lake City. The beautifully landscaped grounds are a tourist attraction in themselves.

81 *(right)* A tourist train, Old Salty, pauses in front of the newly restored Union Pacific Train Station in Salt Lake City.

82 *(left)* The rich Era of the Railroads is memorialized in this stained glass window in the Union Pacific Train Station.

83 The imposing, copper-domed Utah Capitol is one of the most visible buildings in Salt Lake City. The building, patterned after the nation's Capitol, was built of Utah granite in 1912.

84 *(left)* The Great Salt Lake is world-famous for its purple and rose-colored sunsets.

85 Lights flicker on in Salt Lake City's downtown business district as the sun sets in the west.